ELLA HICKSON

Ella Hickson is an award-winning writer whose work has ᴜᴄ̣
performed throughout the UK and abroad. Her most recent play,
ANNA, created with Ben and Max Ringham, opened at the
National Theatre in 2019. *The Writer* and *Oil* opened at the
Almeida Theatre in 2018 and 2017 respectively. In 2013–15
Wendy & Peter Pan, adapted from the book by J.M. Barrie,
played to wide acclaim at the Royal Shakespeare Company.
Other credits include *Riot Girls* (Radio 4), *Boys* (Nuffield
Theatre Southampton/Headlong Theatre/HighTide Festival
Theatre), *Decade* (Headlong Theatre/St Katharine Docks), *The
Authorised Kate Bane* (Grid Iron/Traverse Theatre, Edinburgh),
Rightfully Mine (Radio 4), *Precious Little Talent* (Trafalgar
Studios/Tantrums Productions), *Hot Mess* (Arcola
Tent/Tantrums Productions) and *Eight* (Trafalgar
Studios/Bedlam Theatre, Edinburgh). In 2011 Ella was the
Pearson Writer-in-Residence at the Lyric Theatre Hammersmith
and she was the recipient of the 2013 Catherine Johnson Award.
She has been a MacDowell Fellow. She is developing new work
for the National Theatre, the Old Vic and Manhattan Theatre
Club. Her short film *Hold On Me* premiered at the 55th BFI
London Film Festival. She is also developing various projects
for TV and film.

Ella Hickson

THE WRITER

NICK HERN BOOKS
London
www.nickhernbooks.co.uk

A Nick Hern Book

The Writer first published as a paperback original in Great Britain in 2018
by Nick Hern Books Limited, The Glasshouse, 49a Goldhawk Road, London
W12 8QP

'Quarantine' by Eavan Boland reprinted with the permission of Carcanet Press
Ltd, Manchester, UK and W.W. Norton & Company, Inc, New York

Cover image: Romola Garai, photographed by Clara Giaminardi

Designed and typeset by Nick Hern Books, London
Printed in Great Britain by Mimeo Ltd, Huntingdon, Cambridgeshire PE29 6XX

A CIP catalogue record for this book is available from the British Library

ISBN   978 1 84842 754 9

The Writer was first performed at the Almeida Theatre, London, on 24 April 2018 (previews from 14 April), with the following cast:

ROMOLA GARAI
MICHAEL GOULD
LARA ROSSI
SAMUEL WEST

Direction	Blanche McIntyre
Design	Anna Fleischle
Light	Richard Howell
Sound	Emma Laxton
Video Designer	Zakk Hein
Movement	Sasha Milavic Davies
Casting	Julia Horan CDG
Costume Supervisor	Natasha Prynne
Design Associate	Ruth Hall
Design Assistant	Emily Bestow
Design Intern	Gioia Danz
Resident Director	Piers Black

ALMEIDA
THEATRE

The Almeida Theatre makes brave new work that asks big questions: of plays, of theatre and of the world around us.

Whether new work or reinvigorated classics, the Almeida brings together the most exciting artists to take risks; to provoke, inspire and surprise our audiences.

Recent highlights include *Summer and Smoke* directed by Rebecca Frecknall, *Albion* directed by Rupert Goold, *Ink* directed by Rupert Goold (transferred to the West End), *Hamlet* directed by Robert Icke (transferred to the West End and was broadcast on BBC Two) and Robert Icke's new adaptation of *Mary Stuart* (transferred to the West End and toured the UK).

Past notable productions have included *American Psycho: a new musical thriller* (transferred to Broadway); *Chimerica* (won five Olivier Awards and transferred to the West End); *King Charles III* (won the Olivier Award for Best New Play, transferred to the West End and Broadway, toured the UK and Sydney, and was adapted into a BAFTA nominated TV drama); *Oresteia* (transferred to the West End and won the Olivier Award for Best Director).

Matthew Needham and Patsy Ferran in *Summer and Smoke* by Tennessee Williams, directed by Rebecca Frecknall at the Almeida Theatre (2018). Photo by Marc Brenner.

Artistic Director **Rupert Goold**

Executive Director **Denise Wood**

Associate Director **Robert Icke**

almeida.co.uk

🐦 @AlmeidaTheatre

📘 /almeidatheatre

📷 @almeida_theatre

Registered charity no. 282167

Principal Partner

Supported using public funding by
**ARTS COUNCIL
ENGLAND**

**LONDON THEATRE
OF THE YEAR 2018**
THE STAGE AWARDS

A S P E N

Acknowledgements

I wrote this play at The MacDowell Colony in the summer of 2017. I'd like to thank MacDowell for the space, time and freedom to write. Whilst there I met some brilliant artists who helped me hash out the ideas in this play; Liza Birkenmeier, MT Connolly, Emily Hass, Lisa Kelly, Katherine Behar, Josh Kryah, Asa Horvitz, Alex Tanner and Stephen Karam.

Courage is not a straightforward thing; the kindness of Sacha Wares, Natalie Abrahami, Tanya Seghatchian, Carrie Cracknell, Jenny Worton, Julia Horan and the enduring support of Rachel Taylor have been crucial. I am very grateful.

My thanks to Henry and Fiona Fleet, Nick and Minna Payne and Al and Des Smith for offering home; desks to write at, beds to sleep in, home-cooked meals, babies to hug and miles to run.

Thank you to Oli B, Sam, Jamie, Caitlin, Alice B, Munby, Hutson, Becky Johnson, Douggie McMeekin, Corrigan, Tobes, Jess, Jessie, Izzy, James, Beth, Fran, Jo, Polly and my family for their ears.

My thanks to David Greig for a cabin on Rannoch and a fire in a beer can in Green Park.

My thanks to Lucy Pattison and all at the Almeida. My thanks to Rupert for programming it quickly, allowing it to be urgent and for always taking the risk.

A huge thank you to Blanche, Piers, the cast and the creative team for a gorgeously happy, calm and interrogative rehearsal process.

E.H.

For You

Characters

WRITER
DIRECTOR
FEMALE ACTOR/GIRLFRIEND
MALE ACTOR/BOYFRIEND

In the original production, three audience plants were used.

This text went to press before the end of rehearsals and so may differ slightly from the play as performed.

ONE

A bare stage, post-show, worker lights are on. A YOUNG WOMAN *stands and walks on from the audience, takes in the space, there's something sacred. She breathes. Lights come up. Slowly. It's hers, for a moment. From the back of the auditorium an* OLDER MAN, *forties, like he owns the space. She sees him, freezes. He sees her – stops.*

Hi.

Hi.

Do I –

I left my bag, I had to come back for it.

Right. You were in the audience?

Yes.

You shouldn't be on stage.

I just left my bag. Behind. I –

She grabs the backpack and heads offstage. He's confused, watches her go a second.

You saw the show?

Yes.

Did you enjoy it?

What?

If you want to get your bag in future you should ask a member of front-of-house to come in and get it for you. It's health and safety.

Yes, that's fine.

It's policy.

That's fine.

They're weird about it – you're not meant to be in the auditorium unless you're a member of crew, or we're liable.

It seems unlikely I'd forget it twice but if I do – I'll make sure I ask.

Beat.

Did you enjoy the show?

Small beat.

Were you in it?

You'd remember me if I was in it, no?

I don't know, there were a lot of – guys like you. In it.

You didn't like it?

'Like' isn't the right word, I guess.

What is the right word?

Did you write it?

No.

Did you direct it?

No. Did you come on your own?

Yeah. I have to catch the last Tube. I need to go.

You've got ages yet.

She checks her phone, even though she knows she's got at least an hour.

How old are you?

Twenty-four.

What made you come and see it?

Is this an audience survey?

No.

What is it?

–

I'm on the board. I'm not in town a lot, I want to know why
audiences like the work.

You're assuming we like the work?

You came to see it.

You haven't seen it until you've seen it, though, have you?

You didn't like it?

She shrugs.

Will you come up here? It's strange talking to you whilst you're
down there.

I've got to go. I'm going to be late.

It's totally confidential, I'd be grateful for your candour.

She gets up on stage.

Pause.

Two people walking on stage pretending to be two other people
and saying – 'Hi', 'hi' – or worse – much fucking worse,
walking on stage and – (*Beat.*) 'Phil looks uncomfortable in his
skin, beat, Phil fiddles with his lighter but doesn't light the
cigarette, beat' because we all know cigarettes need a licence to
be lit and Cara enters – 'thunderously sexual, beat', whatever
that fucking means, what does that even mean? 'Cara: the sky,
this evening. Pass me the salt.' What sky? What fucking sky?
This evening? It's all dark in here.

I /

/ A miraculous army of – builders, soldiers, scientists, fucking
women in completely unnecessary hot pants move shit about and
we're all meant to think, what? It's the magic hot-panted people
that move fucking furniture around? With the carpet and the little
bits of flesh-coloured tape sticking the mics on – it's like you
actually think that we're meant to think it's real, like we're meant
to think, with the current state of things that a perfectly charming
front room with people being funny is motherfucking real life?

I'm not sure that's /

The world is imploding.

I –

And the actors, man, they've got nothing new, no insides, they just need the job – they know it's pretend so they're living on the applause and applause alone and that is fucking dangerous. That is a perilous way to be. Moving fucking tables about and living on applause for it. You're staring at them thinking 'do what you like', go on, stop saying those lines and doing what he's told you to do, do something you actually like, go on. Do what you *want*; do it to get laid or I don't give a shit, do it whilst galloping across the stage in a fucking thong pretending to be Bambi, do it HOW THE FUCK YOU LIKE – because at least then someone is actually doing it for real. But then you realise, you're like, oh yeah – fuck – you've been saying lines so long you've got no sense of it, you know – the way they make you so fucking scared of age and poverty and joblessness, that wanting things got way too dangerous a while back. So, you're watching all these people move around, moving tables and pretending, totally deaf to the sound of their own wanting. I can't remember the last time I watched a thing that looked even half-alive. Fake hair and new shoes and famous people doing boring things badly and you know, painfully, like in your bones it hurts – and you can smell the money, so you're not believing a fucking second of it.

–

And of course, that comes with a woman in a tight skirt leaning arse-front over a desk for twenty minutes, for no fucking reason. Because it's all part of the same way of seeing so, you know, it's 'sexy' women and 'smart' men – but actually it's this woman being made to present, like some animal and entitlement just dribbling down the front of its suit – but how it's being given to you is old guys saying some fascinating fucking things about time and history. We're sick, you know that? We're sick to the back fucking teeth of hearing from old men, with flaky skin, at weddings, patting the back of your hand gently as they explain what they consider to be the truths of the world, like I share the same truths, like his truth and my truth are anywhere near the fucking same when it's you that gets to make the world and me that's got to live in it.

She gets choked.

Are you okay?

Sure. I'm fine. (*Swallows.*) It's just you come here thinking you're going to watch something that makes you feel something for the first time in... The state the world is in, you wake up and hear the news and find yourself crying into your fucking cereal, I mean actual tears plopping into your Cheerios and so for some reason you come here – because you think here is where there's meant to be hope and you know what, fuck it. Fuck it.

She picks up her bag and goes to head off the stage.

Stop. Wait a second.

What?

Just wait.

She waits. He doesn't speak.

I watched an entire audience get on their feet tonight for a show that had a dog in it.

Yes. I /

/ Real-life babies. Like that's the only pulse we can find. Silent women in hot pants told to sing like canaries in this fucking day and age are you kidding me? With Trump in, with the monstrosities going down, the world is cracking open and what I just saw is meant to heal us? We should be screaming, we should be speaking in tongues, in a fit, in a fucking – rage, naked, raging, arms open, screaming at the sky – There should not be a dog. There should not be a fucking dog. Not unless you're going to cut its fucking tongue out. Silent women in hot pants? Are you fucking kidding me? What way are you looking at the world that that seems okay to you?

Pause.

I see.

Not if you're sanctioning this shit, you don't see, you really don't.

How did you know it was a male director?

I watched the show. Why are you smiling?

I'm not.

You have a bend in your face.

You just seem very, twenty-four. That's all.

Don't be a patronising cunt.

Jesus.

Beat.

It's done very well at the box office.

Of course it has.

It's going into the West End.

Of course it is.

The critics have loved it.

And in what other realm of life would a twenty-four-year-old woman let a bunch of old white guys tell her what's good to do on a Friday night? Let alone what might defibrillate her soul.

Defibrillate?

Are you laughing?

No. I'm not.

You shouldn't ask somebody to tell you how they feel if you're going to laugh at them.

You're just – very. Impassioned.

And that's funny?

No. It's not. It's… defibrillating.

Long pause.

He doesn't do anything – she doesn't know what to do. She picks up her bag and makes for the door.

Will you wait a second? I'd like to talk to you.

She turns back and looks at him.

What do you do?

I'm a student.

Of?

English. Books.

Yes. I know what /

/ Sure.

Have you ever written anything? That isn't an essay?

I'm not interested in writing for theatre.

Why?

It doesn't work.

What do you mean?

Did you see that play about the posh blokes? You know the one
about those fucking horrendous unforgivably entitled
Cambridge boys –

I think it was Oxford.

Where they were trashing everything and being cruel to people?

I know the one you mean.

I went to see it and I was surrounded, in the audience, by the
same guys that were on stage and they were roaring, they were
fucking loving it. I kept thinking this poor writer. All that rage,
trying to fucking say something, you write your anger down to
get it heard and the people that turned your stomach are loving
it. How sure have you got to be of your power that you enjoy
watching people taking a pop at you? That having people
express their rage about how angry you make them is your idea
of entertainment?

Long pause.

I suppose opposition can be invigorating.

Sure, when it's a hobby.

It was a comedy. I think –

What else was she supposed to do? Shake her fist and be very stern? Because then they'd listen?

I'm sure on some level they /

/ I'm sure on some level they gave zero fucks and carried on doing exactly what they were doing before. Because that's what we let happen. That's how it goes.

Who?

You.

You said we.

The money, the systems, the secret longing to keep it all in place.

Beat.

Could you write something?

What?

For this stage. I think you should write something for this theatre. I think what you have to say is interesting and we should put it on stage.

You get to decide that, do you?

I can talk to the Artistic Director. We'd pay you properly, of course.

You get to hand out money to strangers?

Is that a no?

It'd just be some show.

What do you mean?

People would laugh and give zero fucks and carry on doing exactly what they were doing before.

What else do you want?

I want the world to change shape.

He laughs softly, half-patronising – half-beguiled.

I'm not sure theatre can /

/ So where am I meant to take that impulse? Because I'm very serious about the endeavour.

Small pause.

Maybe this could be a – step in the right direction?

A couple of hundred middle-class folk, here to appease their soul for a few hours so they can enjoy the gin and trot on home?

You're middle-class yourself, no?

Aren't we all these days?

No, I think there are some devastatingly poor people living pretty nearby.

There aren't loads of them in here though, are there?

Beat.

You're also here, on your own, on a Friday seeing a show you purport /

/ Purport?

To hate. So, something's keeping you here.

Beat – she stares at him.

I don't trust it.

What?

I'm going to write books.

Books?

So, it's mine. So, you can just say it. And no one fucks about with it, with their fucking say-so and hedge-betting – I just want to be really clear.

I think you'll find editors definitely have notes to give that will be keeping an eye on what people will buy. Either way what you want to say isn't going to get heard unless it can be sold.

That makes me feel sick. That makes me want to die.

I'm sure it does. But that's how it goes. That's how it is in the world. In this world.

As I said. I want the world to change shape.

It won't.

She breathes heavy, livid.

–

Do you think there should be artists that don't have to think about what people will buy? Do you think there were artists in history that didn't have to think about what people would buy and it made them the ones that saved us when our souls needed saving?

Yes.

And?

Good luck finding one that's willing to run a building.

Why?

It's ninety-per-cent donor dinners, budget sheets and discussions about the toilets.

Doesn't this place get given money by the Government, money that means it should be able to make art.

Yes, some but not a lot these days. So, it's still, mostly, an attempt to get bums on seats.

Do you think the guy that runs this place calls himself an artist?

He laughs.

Is that embarrassing?

I –

Isn't he an Artistic Director?

I think he would refer to himself as a practitioner. He makes work.

There is nothing mythic in this city, is there?

Pause – he stares at her, some quality shifts in the air.

I don't want to ask you again because if it's going to be any good you've got to want to do it.

Beat – she stares at him.

Do you?

What?

Want to? Write something for us?

How do you know I can write?

You can speak and writing is just speaking on paper. There are other people your age who would be biting my arm off for /

/ So, ask them.

I don't want to ask them. They're not angry. They just want the job. Every time they pretend to be angry you can tell they're secretly just doing it because they think angry will get them the job.

Jesus.

What?

And so you're dismissive about their desperation? The job is all they're fucking allowed to want!

They're not as angry as you.

And my anger will get bums on seats.

Honestly? Yes. It's zeitgeisty.

It all feels impossibly defeating. In every direction. It's all so – fucking – (*Looks away.*)

I'm offering you the stage. You don't think you could do anything with that?

It's all so far inside the system – the whole thing is so co-opted that –

I'm not sure I follow.

There was an extra rape.

What?

In tonight's show. The director; tell him – from me, he added a rape. It wasn't in the script. I checked. He added a rape.

–

And why do you think he did that?

Middle-aged male director's go-to for dramatic intensity – I guess.

I don't think he's middle-aged.

I'm not sure that's the point I was making.

You don't agree.

With?

Rape being an act of dramatic intensity?

Sure. It's pretty intense.

But you don't think it should have been included?

I don't see an awful lot of blokes getting fucked in the arse for dramatic flair.

You don't think – at some level, that's what people want to see?

Excuse me?

Well it's been a staple of successful theatre for centuries and people keep coming.

You watch what you're offered.

You don't think there should be sex on stage?

I didn't say sex, I said rape.

What kind of sex is okay?

There was this one show where in the text, you read this moment where a woman pours a glass of water down her front, she's wearing a white T-shirt, and when you read it, it's this real power move, she sexually intimidates the guy by doing it.

When you watched it on stage, she just looked humiliated. She
was owning it the best she could, she committed like hell but
a couple of hundred people staring at your tits, you can't be
master of that. It's looking that does it. I walk on stage; first
thing people think is – how old is she? How hot is she? How
fuckable is she? You walk on stage – they think – what's he got
to say? What's he going to *do*?

So, what do we do about that?

Dismantle capitalism and overturn the patriarchy.

I see. But in the short to medium term?

Dismantle capitalism and overturn the patriarchy.

He laughs.

I do wish you'd stop laughing at things that are perfectly
fucking serious.

It's a grand ambition.

Do you believe in it?

What?

Do you believe that the patriarchy exists? That there is a power
structure in place, in this society, that seeks to systematically
oppress women?

I –

And that you are part of that?

I –

You don't think it exists?

I think. I think young women are angry for a lot of different
reasons and I think one of those reasons is that they feel
disenfranchised but I'm not sure that that's any different from
say issues with poverty or class or race or –

But as a man, do you recognise yourself, in the mirror, as
a power-holder?

Pause.

Do you have a boyfriend?

Brilliant. That is brilliant.

I just mean – I – I'm just interested how this position – your – how this political stance operates in – your – personal life.

There are men that get it.

And that's your boyfriend?

She shrugs.

Do you dominate him?

–

–

You aren't going to answer?

Should I be answering that?

I thought we were having a grown-up conversation about sexual politics. You raised the subject of rape and now, suddenly, you're pretending you're coy. It feels a bit – tricksy.

–

Do you dominate your wife?

Very good.

I imagine you do. I imagine she's younger, less intelligent and heavy into her aesthetics. So that the majority of her status is tied to the ever-ticking time bomb of youth making it feel confusingly inevitable for you when you fuck someone ten years younger in five years' time... if you haven't already.

You're above aesthetics then?

I try not to place my value there.

You could try a little humility.

You're right, I don't think young women have enough of that.

I'm not sure they do these days.

Jesus Christ.

Being oppositional to everything, all the time, being so aggressive – all the time, undermines your argument. Take the note.

I'm not putting together a 'convincing argument'. I'm saying
what I believe to be true.

You don't find older men attractive?

What?

Indulge me.

You are nothing but indulged.

Why don't you find older men attractive?

I find the fact that they're attracted to younger women –
repellent.

That's politics, that's not desire. What we want and what we
believe to be right are different things.

No. It's desire.

You can find something sexually attractive even when you find
it politically offensive.

I don't find it offensive. I find it pathetic. The vanity and ego of
older men needing the attention of younger women to prop them
up. It's pathetic and it's very hard to fuck someone out of pity.

You've spent a considerable amount of time with me.

You asked me to.

That didn't mean you had to, I didn't restrain you.

You said you could do something about what was on stage.
That's why I /

/ I'm just saying there's obviously something about sparring
with older men that you clearly enjoy or we wouldn't be here.

If you want to get anything changed in the world it turns out,
sparring with older men, is part of the fucking deal.

Doesn't mean you don't enjoy it.

Trust me, if there was any other way to get things done – I'd do
it that way. (*Picks up her bag and heads for the door.*) I'm
going to get my Tube. You tell the director of that show, from

me, that theatre is sacred, should be – these spaces – communal and civic and made to heal us when it's – when it's – and he's using it to reinforce his – he's using it to get off on things. And it makes me –

Angry. Yes, I can see that.

She starts to storm off. She stops. She turns around.

–

You don't recognise me, at all, do you?

–

Should I?

Yes.

Student drama festival in Hull. Six years ago. I was eighteen. I'd written one of the pieces. We were on a panel together at the end of the week.

You and I?

You and me.

And?

I spoke about how we'd marketed the show I'd done. You said – 'The idea that the next generation of theatre-makers think theatre should be entertainment, a product to be sold, is evidence of the cultural death of a country. Theatre must speak in opposition to the dominant cultural or ideological forces of the time. It must be insurgent, at best, a revolution.'

It stayed with you.

That's why I keep coming back to watch shows here. I keep hoping you might stick to your word.

You know I directed tonight's show.

Yes, I know you directed tonight's show.

And you think that's okay? To speak to someone, like you just spoke to me, about their work, about the quality of their work?

I wasn't talking about its quality. I was talking about its politics.

It felt like you were talking about its quality.

That's because you see the show as a representation of whether you personally – are talented or not – rather than seeing a play as a statement of politics. A formal expression of a political statement. You are not skewed toward a systemic awareness. I'd say. You're more a – good-night-out – kinda guy.

Pause.

After the panel, you asked me if I wanted to go to the pub and of course, you being who you are and me being eighteen and totally fucking in awe of you – I said yes.

Hm.

And we sat, in this incredible pub, with dark wood and red wine and you told me that writing has to be about truth. That it's holy fire – that these spaces are where we come to scream the things we can't find a way to say in real life.

I said that?

You said that and I felt like… from that day on – I made it, writing, my religion.

Beat.

He takes a step towards her.

You asked to see a bit of my writing, in the pub, and you read it and you said it was good. That I was the real deal, that you could tell with writers, that they either had it or they didn't and you said I might, just, with enough work be good.

–

And you offered me a job. You said I could come and work in your theatre. That you'd find a way for me to get a bit of money so I could develop my voice, that I could write my first full-length play and you'd do everything you could to help me get heard.

–

Why – um – why – didn't you, you never. You haven't worked here.

No.

You didn't take up the offer?

Why?

Because right after you offered me the job – you tried to kiss me. Mid-March. The King's Head. You ate duck. I ordered Scotch to look like a grown-up and never touched it.

–

Your hair was different.

Sure.

Pause.

And you asked if I'd go back to your hotel with you. And you explained that you were married but that wasn't a problem as there was some sort of arrangement – as if your being married was in any way the devastating thing about what you'd just done.

Pause.

What do you mean, devastating? You turned me down.

What?

You rejected me?

I wanted to believe that I was a good writer.

You were good, that's why I offered you a job.

You also tried to kiss me.

They're separate things.

Not to someone that isn't sure why they're in the room.

It wasn't a room, it was a pub.

It was your suggestion to go there.

We talked about sex. We talked about – I remember there being a conversation about – I wouldn't have just, I would have had some sense that /

/ as a – as a thing to do with the work. As a – the human
condition – that's what artists talk about. Writers can discuss
sex without /

/ Well you can forgive me for getting confused? No?

I was eighteen. You were thirty-odd.

I didn't know you were eighteen /

/ It was a student /

/ So what if you were eighteen? There's nothing wrong in that.
You're clearly mature for your age, you're high-handed enough
that I probably thought you were fucking fifty.

I wanted to get that job because I was talented, not because
I was fuckable.

You can be both. You'd think someone might be grateful for
having so many strings to their /

/ You don't see it? You don't fucking see it, at all, do you? The
guys that sit in the meeting and get offered the job don't *ever*,
not for one second do they have to doubt why they're being
given it – they just know it's because they're good.

The guys wouldn't make it to the pub. I wouldn't read their
writing. I wouldn't offer them the job. They're at a disadvantage.

If they do get the job they don't walk around for the next
decade wondering whether their entire career was based on
some married guy wanting to get laid.

Move yourself out of the child position – stop playing the
victim – that I'm not even sure you were – and prove me wrong
for underestimating you. You should have taken the job.

I would have been compromised.

Why?

The women that call you a cunt behind your back are the same
women that wear the short skirts into your meeting room –
I can't be one of those women and make work that feels true to
my bones.

You were excited. I could tell – in that pub – you were excited.

Of course, I was excited.

Was that true to your bones? Right. So, you could have written about how excited you were. That's a play I'd watch.

You can't write from a place of – of – of – (*Tries to catch her breath.*)

That's your own lack of confidence, that's not my /

/ That is the systemic problem with women not feeling like they have anything interesting to say. They think, and god knows why, they're much more valuable for being pretty and fuckable!

I don't see what the problem is with finding a smart beautiful woman attractive?

I could have written things in the last six years that might have changed the world. And I didn't. I didn't because the one person that told me I might be a real artist – also tried to fuck me.

I don't think you can lay your failure at my door. You need to take responsibility for your own insecurity. You shouldn't need my approval.

Pause – she doesn't speak.

–

–

WRITER *and* DIRECTOR *enter. They should be older and slightly less attractive versions of their stage selves. The actor that previously played the* WRITER *becomes* FEMALE ACTOR, *the actor that previously played the* DIRECTOR *becomes* MALE ACTOR.

Everyone gets chairs.

All four sit silently for a second – they look to one another – who will start to speak.

WRITER. Uh – yeah, shall I?

DIRECTOR. Yep, yeah.

WRITER. Uh – so this is just a – work-in-progress. It was something I wrote – and uh, we did this reading just to get a sense of whether it has legs or – um. If it might be something – I might take forward or... uh...

WRITER *looks to* DIRECTOR *who doesn't say anything.*

So... so we thought we'd do this short Q and A afterwards, just to uh. Get a sense of that. We don't want to take up loads of your time, just if there was anything. Anyone. I guess.

FEMALE ACTOR. I thought it was great. I really enjoyed doing it. It sort of did something to my body.

DIRECTOR. You know, obviously, it's got real punch – I think we, I mean I really commend it for that. I think it's got real – uh. It's urgent, but I guess the question is, you know – that's not a play unto itself – that's not enough of a play, just like that – so we'll need to get a sense of where it's going next. It's maybe not enough to just – you know, scream and shout.

WRITER. It needs to affect change.

DIRECTOR. Right.

WRITER. That was a big worry in writing it, in fact. You know that concern about being, I mean she's twenty-four, she's you know, young – but still the anger – is pretty relentless.

DIRECTOR. Certainly is.

Nervous laughter.

WRITER. You get stuck between this – you know moany-victim place or angry-woman place – and it doesn't feel you can get heard anywhere in between.

DIRECTOR. In its defence, there's some pretty well-structured argument in there too.

WRITER. Right, so argument is where it's heard but if you wanted to be impassioned, there's only two positions available. Argument, you know, formally – is pretty, it's his side of things. They're the terms he wants to be on.

DIRECTOR. But as I said, the argument is good. We had to work hard on that. It was a real outpouring when we first got it.

WRITER. I guess that's how anger /

DIRECTOR. / And we really had to knock it into shape. It desperately needed rigour and logic – the parts where it gets – you know, ranty – it can become insufferable.

WRITER. I think she's just trying to get heard.

DIRECTOR. Right, and we've had to do quite a lot of work on it structurally, to make sure that is the case.

WRITER *raises her eyebrows slightly, tense smile.*

WRITER. Sure.

DIRECTOR. You don't think?

WRITER. I'm not sure it's better – I think it's just – I guess there are different forms of expression and some of them are more easily – understood than others.

DIRECTOR. You think what you originally sent in was more comprehensible?

WRITER. In a sense.

DIRECTOR. You're out of your mind.

WRITER. Its structure was formed through instinct. It might not have been logically /

DIRECTOR. It was a mess.

WRITER. According to your idea of structure.

FEMALE ACTOR. I liked the first draft. It was – mad. It was fucking great to do. It was all over the place.

DIRECTOR. Exactly.

MALE ACTOR. I really liked it as well.

WRITER. Horses for courses.

DIRECTOR. This is a better piece of writing.

WRITER. Depending on your definition of better. Shall we take another question?

DIRECTOR. If you think this version is self-indulgent you should have seen the first draft.

WRITER. I'm not sure emotive, personal expression and self-indulgence are necessarily the same thing. I find fifteen pages of finely wrought, cold, rational, academic dialectic self-indulgent. Just because it's a woman standing on stage saying how she feels /

DIRECTOR. / How *she feels*, exactly. This entire movement at the moment is so fucking self–

WRITER. As opposed to how *he thinks*. You don't think we're saturated with how 'he thinks'. I mean the entire structure of the Western world is organised on the principle of how 'he thinks'.

DIRECTOR. Exactly 'the world' – it's a broader perspective, it's accessible to – it's not just one person's endless, self-involved perspective on their own anguish.

WRITER. Hamlet.

DIRECTOR. Which uses the personal as a political /

WRITER. / So why can't the same be true here?

FEMALE ACTOR. It doesn't feel like a rant – to play it.

Weird – long pause – no one seems to have an answer.

DIRECTOR. Any more questions from the audience?

AUDIENCE PLANT. Have you been able to have the conversation you have in the play with any of the practitioners you work with in real life?

Beat.

WRITER. Is that for me?

DIRECTOR. Obviously.

WRITER. It could be for you –

DIRECTOR. I didn't write it.

WRITER. Um – there, uh – most of our conversation has been dramaturgical. I mean – that's the /

DIRECTOR. / The work is the thing that matters. That's what we're here to develop. Any more questions?

AUDIENCE PLANT. This is for – well, I guess everyone. Do you think it's weird that your character talks about power so much and being a woman but doesn't mention race?

DIRECTOR. Good question and it's something we consider in every show we do – we make sure that casting is representative of a level of diversity that – you've worked here before, haven't you?

FEMALE ACTOR. Uh-huh. Yeah. I – love working here.

WRITER. But I totally acknowledge that the play doesn't really deal with it. Like, I didn't want to be glib but – also – um, it's not about race. Although power – I mean, is always about – I take some – I admit that – sorry.

FEMALE ACTOR. It's a great part. It's a better – I'm just glad we're having the, I really love the play.

MALE ACTOR. I think it's really fascinating. We've been really mindful in the room. We've had a lot of fascinating conversations about intersectionality and voicelessness and how little people feel they can say – I didn't actually.

FEMALE ACTOR (*smiles at him, she's taking the piss*). Yeah, I know.

DIRECTOR. Shall we take another question?

AUDIENCE PLANT. When you were trying to turn it from the sort of outpouring into the more logical argument – how did you decide what stays and what goes?

WRITER *looks at* DIRECTOR, DIRECTOR *looks at* WRITER. *Pause.*

WRITER. We had to make it about what was happening between the two characters. We had to interrogate what they were doing *to* each other.

AUDIENCE PLANT. And what are they doing to each other? Do you think?

MALE ACTOR. I think it's complex.

FEMALE ACTOR. There's a lot of shifting about I guess.

MALE ACTOR. But on the whole. I think the idea is /

WRITER. / I think the director sees the potential in the writer for a good show and I think he exploits that potential. Sorry, I didn't mean to interrupt.

DIRECTOR. And the writer wants to be heard and yet isn't doing any listening herself.

WRITER. I think she's done her fair share of listening.

Beat. Then everyone looks to the WRITER *who doesn't say anything.*

FEMALE ACTOR. I'm just thinking who actually gets what they want? In that sense, who is the protagonist. I mean she can't put the play on by herself – so /

WRITER. / She needs his permission.

Long pause.

DIRECTOR. Okay, great – that's great – there's a man at the back waving his hand in the air which I think is our cue to shut up.

Everyone clears their chairs away.

FEMALE ACTOR *and* MALE ACTOR *clear the space.* DIRECTOR *goes to leave,* WRITER *stops him.*

WRITER. What shall I…

DIRECTOR. Hm?

WRITER. What's the – will it, um. What's next?

DIRECTOR. When can you get the rest of it to me?

WRITER. Uh. I –

DIRECTOR. The sooner you can get it to me.

DIRECTOR *exits*.

TWO

BOYFRIEND, *mid-thirties, eligible. A naturalistic set of a young, arty, intellectual, urban couple's front room is moved on around him, constructed by stage management (all female), who arrange it around him, like mothers. A chair moves beneath him and he sits, a beer on a side table. On the back wall of the sitting room is an A3 poster for a show titled* ANGRY YOUNG WOMAN – *it features the face of the* WRITER, *looking slightly distraught/sexy – in a pink wig with mascara smeared down her face. The 'naturalistic' sitting room should feature a table and chairs, and soft lighting. Last of all, a brand-new sofa is moved into the sitting room. It's smart, classy – maybe a bit Swedish but probably John Lewis.* BOYFRIEND, *who was being made a little uncomfortable by the playscript he was reading, loves it. It's his favourite new thing, top end.*

WRITER *enters, wearing a coat, it's been raining out, the coat/*WRITER *has been sprayed with water – she shakes out a wet umbrella.*

BOYFRIEND. Shit, no. Go out again.

WRITER. Really?

BOYFRIEND. Please?

WRITER. Ufh.

The WRITER *exits back through the same door. The* BOYFRIEND *picks up a party popper that he's prepared earlier and waits by the door.*

BOYFRIEND. Go!

Nothing happens. BOYFRIEND *reaches for the door to open it,* WRITER *opens it at the same time. It slightly hits* BOYFRIEND *in the face.*

WRITER. Fuck. Sorry.

BOYFRIEND (*recovering quickly not wanting to miss the moment*). Waheey!

> BOYFRIEND *pops the party popper in* WRITER's *face – it makes her jump a bit.*

WRITER. Shit.

> BOYFRIEND *grabs her, kisses her, spins her round. It's romantic. They kiss – it's happy.*

> What are we doing?

BOYFRIEND. Celebrating.

WRITER. What?

BOYFRIEND. You.

WRITER. What is that?

BOYFRIEND. A sofa.

WRITER. Why?

BOYFRIEND. I bought us a new sofa.

WRITER. Huh.

BOYFRIEND. It's the one you wanted.

WRITER. Is it?

BOYFRIEND. Oh shit, ah – wait.

> BOYFRIEND *goes to the drawer he got the party popper from, takes a handful of glitter confetti and lobs it in the* WRITER's *face.*

WRITER. Ah.

BOYFRIEND. Yeah.

WRITER. Confetti. Yahoo.

BOYFRIEND. Yahoo.

WRITER. Why are we throwing confetti?

BOYFRIEND. I saw the contract.

WRITER. What contract?

BOYFRIEND. On the table.

WRITER. Oh. What can I smell?

BOYFRIEND. Cassoulet.

WRITER. Fuck off.

BOYFRIEND. Fuck on.

WRITER. I love cassoulet.

BOYFRIEND. I know.

> BOYFRIEND *starts kissing* WRITER. *It takes her slightly by surprise. She stumbles backwards.* BOYFRIEND *leads her back onto/over to the sofa and pushes her back until she's lying down on it.* WRITER *disappears from view.*

WRITER. Can I take my coat off?

BOYFRIEND. No.

WRITER. Why not?

BOYFRIEND. It makes you look like a grown-up. I feel like I'm fucking a grown-up.

> *The way the sofa is arranged we can't see the sex – we can only see the person 'on top' – whoever is beneath is obscured by the sofa back. She doesn't make much noise, he does – he comes – she doesn't. They finish – he stands up. She sits up still in her coat.*

Shit, the cassoulet.

> BOYFRIEND *runs through to the kitchen.*

> WRITER *spots the script on the side. She picks it up sees how far through he is, puts it back down. As she does so he comes back through with bottle of wine and two glasses.*

You can take it off now.

WRITER. What?

BOYFRIEND. The coat.

WRITER. It's okay.

BOYFRIEND. Take it off.

WRITER. Why?

BOYFRIEND. You're inside. You don't wear a coat inside.

WRITER. I'm kind of cold.

BOYFRIEND. Take it off. It's weird to wear a coat inside. You look strange.

WRITER. It's fine.

BOYFRIEND. We're about to eat. I've made a really nice meal. I've got wine. It's Tempranillo. Take your coat off.

Small beat. WRITER *takes off the coat.*

It's serious money.

BOYFRIEND *pours the wine.*

WRITER. What is?

BOYFRIEND. The contract.

BOYFRIEND *hands* WRITER *the glass.*

WRITER. I'm not going to do it.

BOYFRIEND *retracts the glass.*

BOYFRIEND. What?

WRITER. They sent it over to try and persuade me with the money. I've already decided I'm not going to do it.

BOYFRIEND. It's forty grand.

WRITER *shrugs. Takes the wine from* BOYFRIEND *and drinks some.*

You've already written the play, you just need to turn it into a film.

WRITER. I don't want to do it.

BOYFRIEND. I'll do it.

She laughs. It's a bit louder than she intended. He does not laugh.

Do you know how long it would take me to make that money?

WRITER. A year.

BOYFRIEND. And this would take you?

WRITER. I don't want to do it. I don't need to do it. We're fine as we are. Is that why you bought the sofa?

BOYFRIEND. It's a present. You wanted the sofa.

WRITER. A sofa? I don't think I've ever wanted a sofa.

BOYFRIEND. You said, when we were at Jo and Pete's – you pointed at it and said, 'nice sofa'.

WRITER. We were making shit up.

BOYFRIEND. What?

WRITER. Jo was talking about cake, you were talking about the guy at work called Yan who makes everyone call him Jan because it's easier and Pete was putting banana into the kid.

BOYFRIEND. Alex.

WRITER. What?

BOYFRIEND. The child is called Alex.

WRITER. I know that.

BOYFRIEND. How is putting food into a child making things up?

WRITER. He was making aeroplane noises. I was just saying words.

Beat.

BOYFRIEND. Right.

BOYFRIEND *goes out through to the kitchen.*

WRITER. Are you okay? I didn't mean to make you angry. I didn't know you loved sofas.

BOYFRIEND *comes back out with the cassoulet.*

BOYFRIEND. I thought you loved sofas. It was a present. It was nearly two thousand pounds.

WRITER. What is wrong with you?

BOYFRIEND. What's wrong with me?

WRITER. Who spends two thousand pounds on a sofa?

BOYFRIEND. I thought it was nice.

WRITER. I just don't want to do the job. That's okay for me not to want to do it.

BOYFRIEND. Do you want some cassoulet?

WRITER. Sure.

BOYFRIEND. More red wine?

WRITER. Sure.

BOYFRIEND. I've got chocolate for after.

WRITER. That sounds delicious.

BOYFRIEND. You could say thank you?

WRITER *looks affronted.* BOYFRIEND *goes back into the kitchen.*

WRITER. Thank you.

BOYFRIEND *comes back out of the kitchen with sweet potato.*

The sweet potato is an amazing colour.

BOYFRIEND. I wouldn't bother eating it, it probably tastes like shit.

WRITER. Why are you being /

BOYFRIEND. / Don't force it down if you don't want it. I don't want you putting anything in your mouth against your will.

WRITER. We didn't even know about that job yesterday and we were perfectly fine.

BOYFRIEND. I've got a fucking apron on.

WRITER. So, take it off.

BOYFRIEND. I don't want to get cassoulet on my shirt because I have to wear it to work tomorrow so I can go and do my job that I don't like.

WRITER. Can you articulate exactly what it is that I've done wrong?

BOYFRIEND. People have to do their jobs. That's what happens. You get a job and you have to do it.

WRITER. You don't have to do your job if you don't want to.

BOYFRIEND. But we've got rent to pay. So, I'd best continue to sort out the logistics for shipping football boots around the world.

WRITER. I pay the same rent you do.

BOYFRIEND. We need to buy a house.

WRITER. We didn't need to buy a house yesterday.

BOYFRIEND. I don't understand why you wouldn't take that job. I would take that job in a flash.

WRITER. I know.

BOYFRIEND. Meaning?

WRITER. You can't be offended that I've 'insinuated' that you would take the job. You just said you would take the job.

BOYFRIEND. Why won't you do it?

WRITER (*matter-of-fact*). Because the story I wrote, when I wrote it, was true. The thing I said was true. And if I turn it into a film the producers will break it and and smash it and twist it into this thing that isn't true and that will hurt.

BOYFRIEND. It's a story.

WRITER. But. Doesn't matter.

BOYFRIEND. No, go on, try to explain. I'm listening to you.

WRITER. Letting producers they – it feels like letting strangers do plastic surgery to your unborn child to make it more fuckable.

BOYFRIEND. Vivid.

WRITER. And when they're done fucking it and it comes out dead, dead and blue and limp they can't understand why there's no love or life or faith or magic in your story and so they ask you to do it again, but this time could you put more heart into it and when you say no, they offer you money – more and more money, like that's the thing that is going to make you let someone fuck your kid.

BOYFRIEND. It's a job. It's how you make your money. There's rent to pay.

WRITER. I've covered your rent three times this year and never once asked you to cover mine.

BOYFRIEND. You ever going to let that go?

WRITER. Shall we finish our meal?

BOYFRIEND. You're not going to just write plays forever.

WRITER. Aren't I?

BOYFRIEND. You'll be poor.

WRITER. Were you hoping your investment was going to mature?

BOYFRIEND. I –

WRITER. You're always going to ship things.

BOYFRIEND. I'll get promoted. I'm getting promoted.

WRITER. That's great.

BOYFRIEND. Don't say it like that, it is great.

WRITER. I said it like it was actually great.

BOYFRIEND. Who doesn't want to get promoted?

WRITER. What do you *mean* promoted? I'm a writer?

BOYFRIEND. To films, to films! To forty fucking grand –
that is a promotion. Take the promotion. No one says no to
a promotion.

WRITER. I don't want it!

BOYFRIEND. Why not? Is it a lack of confidence? Is it
because you don't believe you can do it?

WRITER. No, it's because I am already rich and livid and
thumping with magic and myth and a deep-seated sense of
purpose about what I have to do to try and change the world
before I die.

He looks at her like she's insane, is she taking the piss?

BOYFRIEND. Why do you have to be weird? Like
intentionally fucking weird. It's so boring being so fucking
alternative all the time.

Beat.

WRITER. I'm not with you because of your potential for growth.
I'm not with you because you will become something better.
I'm with you because previous to this episode, you're a good
man. You're a good and kind and sound man, who – when he
has to make decisions – considers them thoroughly from all
perspectives, not just his own. That is why I am with you
because you're fair and kind.

BOYFRIEND. And because you love me?

WRITER. And because I love you.

BOYFRIEND. And because you want to fuck me.

WRITER (*says it but there's a whisper of not being quite
convinced in it*). And because I want to fuck you.

Pause – he won't confront it.

BOYFRIEND. I always have the feeling there is something
you'd rather be doing.

WRITER. I never stop you from doing what you want.

BOYFRIEND. I want you.

WRITER. That's cheating because it involves another person.

BOYFRIEND. Everything involves another person.

WRITER. Does it? Should it?

BOYFRIEND. Shall I just fuck off then?

WRITER. I love you more than anyone.

BOYFRIEND. Thing.

WRITER. What?

BOYFRIEND. Do you love me more than anything?

WRITER (*lie*). Yes.

BOYFRIEND. Did you fuck him?

WRITER. What?

BOYFRIEND. I know it says in the thing that you didn't but –
    just the way you talk about him and your face goes strange
    when you say his name – did you fuck him? The director?
    Even though it says you didn't?

WRITER. I've never fucked him. I never even kissed him.

BOYFRIEND. It says in the thing that you did.

WRITER. I told him to get off and I sent him home to his wife.
    He isn't the point.

BOYFRIEND. What is the point?

WRITER. Don't you ever feel like all this is pretending?

BOYFRIEND. All what?

WRITER. All this –

BOYFRIEND. You're in opposition to everything, all the time.
    Like, if we're with friends or my parents or at a club –
    you're always on the outside pretending you're not part of it.

Saying it's all bullshit. No, I don't think this is pretending.
I think it's real life. And I think you can't handle it. You can't
stay in bed next to me rather than creep down here and write
stories. You can't just do your job without making a drama of
it. It's a cop-out. It's cowardly. It's all so fucking spineless.
You lot with your stages and your stories and your passion
and – it's gross.

WRITER. You want a world with no stories in it?

BOYFRIEND. The night I first met you. You'd just got off the
phone to someone.

WRITER. Had I?

BOYFRIEND. You said you'd just spoken to someone that had
made you feel less lonely for the first time in years. Someone
that made parties bearable. I mean, anyway – it was gone
midnight.

WRITER. Was it?

BOYFRIEND. He'd read you a poem down the phone. I sat and
listened to you say it – you said it out into the woods, like it
was magic or something – 'It was the worst hour of the worst
season' – like you were lost in it and it felt so – urgh – and
I was thinking what the fuck is this guy doing, sitting at
home with his wife and sending poems to young women.

Small beat.

[*No pressure, but just in terms of defending the whole of art,
this should be totally magic.*]

WRITER. In the worst hour of the worst season
   of the worst year of a whole people
   a man set out from the workhouse with his wife.
   He was walking – they were both walking – north.

   She was sick with famine fever and could not keep up.
   He lifted her and put her on his back.
   He walked like that west and west and north.
   Until at nightfall under freezing stars they arrived.

In the morning, they were both found dead.
Of cold. Of hunger. Of the toxins of a whole history.
But her feet were held against his breastbone.
The last heat of his flesh was his last gift to her.

WRITER *holds her fist against her breastbone.*

We can see a fraction of the DIRECTOR *in the wings.*

WRITER *is looking in his direction, or possibly – just past him.*

BOYFRIEND *is very much in the sitting room and not at all on stage. He tries to take her fist and put it on his chest – the* WRITER *pulls back – doesn't want him to have it, it's not his.*

BOYFRIEND. It's not real.

WRITER. It feels real.

BOYFRIEND. It's escapism.

The sound of a baby crying. It sounds incredibly real and incredibly close.

WRITER. What is that?

BOYFRIEND. I think it's a baby.

BOYFRIEND *re-enters the sitting room.*

The sound of the baby again.

I think it's coming from next door.

WRITER. There is no next door.

BOYFRIEND. What the fuck is wrong with you?

WRITER. Me?

They glare – stand-off – who is going to break it.

The sound of the baby gets louder and louder – it's almost insufferably loud.

BOYFRIEND *doesn't seem to notice how loud it is,* WRITER *can't bear it.*

I'll do the job if you really want me to do the job. I should do the job. It you want me to do it I'll do take the job.

The sound of the baby stops.

BOYFRIEND. I think it's a really good thing to do.

WRITER. Yeah.

BOYFRIEND. You'll be considered as more established. It'll offer you a sense of security for the future.

WRITER. Yeah.

BOYFRIEND. That's not to be scoffed at.

WRITER. I know.

BOYFRIEND. That's what life is.

WRITER. I know.

BOYFRIEND. My girlfriend writes movies.

WRITER. Yeah.

He grabs her excitedly and kisses her. She smiles. They dance a bit – it should be glorious. It's not quite.

I don't know what I'll write but I'll tell them I'll do it – I'll get the money.

BOYFRIEND. You just write the same story as in the play but in a film – the stuff that happens to the girl. You just write it down.

WRITER. She's a woman.

BOYFRIEND. You say boy all the time.

WRITER. The only thing is that I don't want to write it.

BOYFRIEND. Everyone has to do things they don't want to do sometimes.

WRITER. I do things I don't want to do all the time.

BOYFRIEND. Do you? Really? Like what? I can't think of one thing you do that you don't want to do.

WRITER. Go for dinner with your mother. Wear shoes. Eat anything other than cheese on toast. Speak. Have sex with you.

BOYFRIEND. Excuse me?

WRITER. Sometimes I do. Sometimes I don't. That's just how it is – I get that. But writing isn't like that. I can't do it when I don't want to do it. It has to be the wanting. Or it feels like death. Like I'm breaking.

BOYFRIEND. Whereas sleeping with me when you don't want to feels like?

WRITER. Going to the gym, I'm always glad I've gone afterwards. Once it's done.

BOYFRIEND. Jesus fucking Christ.

WRITER. That's honest.

BOYFRIEND. Just because it *feels* honest to you – doesn't give you the right to say it out loud. Just because it's fucking true doesn't mean you get to say it. Other people have feelings. Truth is not carte blanche. Do you get that?

WRITER. I'm sorry.

BOYFRIEND. What for?

WRITER. I don't know but I feel like I should say it.

BOYFRIEND *starts aggressively tidying*.

Imagine Picasso painting a picture he didn't want to paint. How do you even do that? Paint what you don't want to paint. Do you get it?

BOYFRIEND. YOU ARE NOT PICASSO. YOU WILL NEVER BE PICASSO. STOP THINKING YOU ARE FUCKING PICASSO. IT IS DIGUSTING.

BOYFRIEND *takes the pot of cassoulet and upturns it on top of* WRITER*'s laptop – so it's totally submerged. He opens it – and dumps the sweet potato on the keyboard, just to make sure*.

WRITER *stares a moment.*

WRITER *exits. She walks out of the apartment door and onto the side of the stage. We can see her on the stage but not inside the set. She is desperate with what seems impossible. There is no space.* BOYFRIEND *is inside. He's not quite sure what to do with himself.* BOYFRIEND *stands. He turns up the music. He looks about a moment. He sits down. He drinks from a glass of wine until it's empty and then keeps taking swigs of it like there's wine still in there. He goes through to the kitchen. He emerges from the kitchen. He goes to the fake window and stares through the window at the blank, theatre wall for some time. He breathes likes the view is giving him freedom.* WRITER *can see him staring.* WRITER *comes back in.*

BOYFRIEND *turns to look at her.*

Pause – they look at each other. It's love. Beneath it all – it's real love and yet –

WRITER. The thing is. I really do love you. Do you get that? That I find it almost impossible to live like this /

BOYFRIEND. / Thanks.

WRITER. I feel like I can't breathe most of the time.

BOYFRIEND. That makes me feel great.

WRITER. It's physically painful, a lot of the time, when we have friends over and I hold champagne and I go to bed after and pretend that I'm sleeping. And I do it every single day even though it makes my skin itch. And in a way, you can get away with loving me less.

BOYFRIEND. What?

WRITER. Because you genuinely enjoy a sofa. And I know that sounds elitist and bit cunty and I sound like a narcissistic prick but there are cheerful people who sit all day and watch TV and love it. You are never happier than in the exotic-foods aisle at Waitrose selecting a new selection of snacking nuts and sometimes, I stand there, with the trolley and I feel like I'm dissolving inside just watching your capacity for happiness. And in me, for some reason, snacking nuts, exotic or otherwise, don't stop this constant need for something – bigger – all the time. I want awe. I feel like I need blood. All the time. And anything less than that makes me feel desperate. It makes me feel like I want to die. Either I can feel real but I'm living in a world of cartoons or you and the world are real and I feel like I go see-through. And it's not like that for you. You have snacking nuts. You're perfectly happy in the world as it is. And it hurts to watch because I want to be like that so badly that it makes me actually hurt to watch you in Waitrose, smiling so much, over those snacking nuts.

Pause.

He approaches her – he takes her face in his hands – he kisses her.

She kisses him back.

It's real love.

BOYFRIEND. Don't do the job if you don't want to it.

WRITER. Okay.

BOYFRIEND. I just desperately want you to be happy.

WRITER. I know.

BOYFRIEND. I'll keep selling football boots. You don't have to do the job.

WRITER. The two things aren't related.

BOYFRIEND. I'll keep selling football boots for us.

WRITER. I've never lived off your money.

BOYFRIEND. I'll look after you.

WRITER. I think if I can do what I want I might make something incredible.

BOYFRIEND. It might make us a million.

WRITER. It could be amazing.

BOYFRIEND. It might make us a million.

WRITER. That too.

They kiss – beat.

BOYFRIEND. Can I say something?

WRITER. Yes.

BOYFRIEND. Something – true.

WRITER. Yes. Please. Yes, you can.

BOYFRIEND. I was thinking, reading your play how you're a bit like he is, the director – trying to plug yourself into this life force that you're too old for. Still trying to stick your dick in younger, more alive things because you're a coward about growing up. You're like him that you still want awe. Neither of you have realised that it doesn't exist. You both need to grow up.

DIRECTOR *steps into view a little bit.* WRITER *is distracted by him over* BOYFRIEND's *shoulder.*

We've got more than most people, we get on and laugh and help each other solve problems when one of us is sitting in the bath and the other one is sitting on the toilet with the lid closed.

WRITER. Shall I make you a cup of tea?

BOYFRIEND. And you can't see how grateful you should be. You think there's more and you've already got loads. And you're going to waste it from being selfish and you'll always regret it and it will make you sad for the rest of your life that you weren't able to see love and goodness when you had it because you were all the time wanting more and not realising that more doesn't exist.

WRITER *flicks a look at* DIRECTOR.

Not like you think it does. More isn't out there, or over there – it's more by just keeping on with the normal stuff. That's where more is, from the inside out.

BOYFRIEND *gets down on one knee.*

WRITER. Don't do that.

The sound of the baby again – it's quiet first, gurgling and sweet and then it gets louder – not offensively loud this time, it stays small and sweet and gentle. WRITER *is distracted by it.* BOYFRIEND *seems not to be.* BOYFRIEND *takes a ring box out of his back pocket and opens it – and offers the ring up to* WRITER.

Pause.

Get up. Please.

BOYFRIEND. Why?

WRITER. It makes me feel weirdly big. It makes you seem weirdly small.

BOYFRIEND. That's okay.

WRITER. I don't like it. I feel huge. Get up.

BOYFRIEND. It's fine.

WRITER. If you don't get up, I'm worried. I won't want to fuck you any more.

BOYFRIEND *stands up. Puts the ring back in his pocket.*

BOYFRIEND. The guys, the guys down the pub say their girlfriends are biting their hands off to get married.

WRITER. I know.

BOYFRIEND. You'll get older and wish you'd said yes to everything cos it'll be gone. What has 'no' ever actually achieved?

WRITER. I'm not afraid. I'm going to not be afraid. If that's okay with you?

BOYFRIEND. 'As you age past forty, the percentage of the dating pool that is able to form a secure, stable relationship drops to less than thirty per cent.'

WRITER. That sounds like a really unverifiable statistic.

BOYFRIEND. The world doesn't want you odd, you're the only one that's enjoying it.

The baby again – this time it sounds different – like really really real.

BOYFRIEND *goes to the door, opens it, takes a real-life baby off stage management –* the BOYFRIEND *bounces it and makes coo-ing sounds.*

WRITER. That's not our baby.

BOYFRIEND. I think Mummy is just scared. I think Mummy lacks confidence.

WRITER. That's not true.

BOYFRIEND. I think Mummy doesn't want to be happy.

WRITER. I don't know if that would make me happy.

BOYFRIEND. Look at her.

Long pause – she does, the baby's gorgeous – she holds her – so tight, breathes her in, her heart breaks a bit.

WRITER. That child belongs to the woman in the wings.
That child is being paid to be here. Doesn't that strike you as slightly fucked up? Do you want to come and take your child back?

BOYFRIEND. We have a baby.

BOYFRIEND *shows the baby to the* WRITER.

We had a baby.

WRITER. That baby has been bought. It's being paid to be here. I did not give birth to that baby.

WRITER *takes off her shoes.*

BOYFRIEND. Listen to me. We can be happy. We can be happier than you can imagine. Just because you can't imagine it doesn't mean that we can't be happy.

WRITER. I'm sorry. But I've got a really good imagination.

Pause – they stare at each other, the fabric breaks.

The back flat falls down. The shelves start falling apart.

Stage management comes on and start cleaning up the table, it all gets disassembled and wiped clean, put in boxes. Their life and all its potential is packed away, ripped to shreds, it stops existing. As if there is nothing there, was never anything there, like it just can't hold.

The mother of the baby comes and takes the child.

WRITER *flinches a second – not wanting to let go, not wanting to see it disappear – but lets it go.*

BOYFRIEND, *equally – becomes* MALE ACTOR. *He transforms entirely – takes off clothes, a wig – and* WRITER *reaches out for him, to get him back – but he's gone.*

WRITER *staring off the way he went, slightly devastated.*

He exits through the back flats that have fallen down. He goes and has a conversation with costume – they have a flirty giggle together. The real person – the real boyfriend has gone.

The speaker that had the baby crying through it has fallen to the floor and is still wailing – WRITER *bends down and turns the speaker down until it clicks to off.* DIRECTOR *is watching her. Just watching.* WRITER *knows he is there, always there – but doesn't turn to look at him.* WRITER *steps out of costume.*

DIRECTOR *watches.*

WRITER *goes over to the laptop and tries to shake the cassoulet and sweet potato off it. She wipes it clean, licks it off – tries to save it, puts it under her arm. It's precious.*

The DIRECTOR *watches.*

THREE

[*THE PROVOCATION: What follows should be an attempt at staging female experience, the director should be aware of avoiding the inherently patriarchal nature of theatre:*

Female characters should <u>do</u> – they are not having things done to them. Bodies are for action, not titillation or decoration. There should be no looking. The protagonist should own the space.]

I stand, mostly unable to move – exhausted from all the pretending, in a café, staring at an older lady, eating.

    – Do you have a question?
    – Sorry?
    – Can I help you?
    – Um.

    – What are you looking at?
The truth is, her left hand. There's nothing there.
    – It looks like good cake. I say.
She searches my face for something that she isn't finding.
    – Do you want to sit?

I've got an appointment. I want to sit and watch her eat all day. I put my pretzel in the bin and leave.

They don't tell you that having a contraceptive device fitted into your uterus, feels like having the hook of a coat hanger pulled up through your oesophagus whilst you are trying to swallow. It's the alien pain of a foreign object. The cramping that your body does to try and eject the thing makes your mind go black. The nurse has fake nails, squared-off, at least an inch long that are threatening the integrity of the latex gloves. She says she'll do me a favour and cut the strings short so he won't feel them.

I don't see the small step, on the way back into the waiting room. I'd been sick twice with the nurse so thought I was done but now I'm passing out and my hand can't find the floor.

The old woman catches my elbow and brings me back up to standing. I have no idea how she knew to be there.

Out in the cold air, she walks two foot in front of me and tells me to follow.

She's got a mane of grey hair and a cowboy's stride; heading, legs akimbo, down Goodge Street.

They say her name's Semele. That she saw the light and easily survived it. Zeus showed her what he'd got. She had a little laugh and went on her way. Out into the world to collect her daughters. Every one of which she named, Dionysus.

This other mother puts me in a cab and tells me to brace myself against the ceiling and the window so that my newly minted cervix doesn't smash against the seat, she leans in to the driver's window and tells him to avoid the bumps and not to be a dick about it.

We travel a thousand miles and Semele leaves me lake-side.

It's shitting it down and freezing. Semele stops a minute, to sun herself on a lichen-covered rock, then fucks off to collect more daughters. She doesn't check to see if I can swim.
The lake is down below zero. It's a mile out and back.
I'm in a pair of jeans and a slightly crappy tank top. Suddenly there's someone standing next to me. A new arrival. She's in DM boots, a bobble hat and shorts. We're fucked, I think.
She looks at me. I look at her. We take our clothes off. As if it's going to make the slightest bit of difference.

We stand, like posts, our arms wrapped around our waists; silent except for the deafening patter of rain on lake and the quickening of our own breath.
'I can't do it'
'You'll be fine' she says – little and Midwestern. Stating 'fine' like a fact and heavy on the 'be'. 'You'll *be* fine'.
She's small, I'm tall. I wonder if Semele worked it out that way. The Midwesterner has a compact pragmatism about her, that makes me trust.

Suddenly then, me, laughing, fuck it, gasping, fuck it-fuck it-fuck it – fuck it – jesus-fucking-christ – fucking-fuckety-fuckety – fuckety-shit – shit fuck-christ: (*Wading, pushing, splashing, crashing.*) and she's in just after.

[*Spoken or sound design*: *Pshhhsssh – and glub glub glub glub and then she makes a soft guttural rasping of the rain on the surface, glub blub blub. And gasps – she's up for air and the rain is louder and then – gasp and gulp – down again – splash and glub glub glub.*]

There's a panic that you'll never make it to the other side but that's the point.
You're going to die a thousand times, lose sight of shore for days, and with every rasping breath you feel the full weight of all the loss in the world. There is no other way but endless evisceration. Skin and flay and burn and throw it all away again and again and again. Throw yourself overboard so many times that you lose your mind from falling; until you're sick to your stomach of having to trust in things you were raised to find revolting.

(NB, PS – at this time – in the crossing of the river – when shit gets real – false flatterers are the enemy. When you are cutting your teeth on your power, do not – I repeat, do *not*, entertain compliments. Get on with your work. People blowing smoke up your arse can throw you off for years and there isn't time to waste. Only entertain people with edges. Abandon all hope of anything softer and, as I said, get on with your work.)

[*She comes up from the water, a really sharp gasp of air, the rain falling hard on the water.*

Then plunges down again.]

I look behind me, quickly, to see where my mate is. A seal head, a corkscrew leg but steely determination. She's half my size, and totally fucking fine. Her face says look front. So I do and keep swimming, my heart is beating too fast and my lungs won't fill from the cold. I have to forcibly forget that, increasingly, I can't feel my arms.

Push on. We two go like drones, grabbing fists of breath from the air. Our lips go blue. Our hands turn white. I lose my toes entirely so that it takes a minute to realise – when one flailing foot grazes the seabed – that we've arrived.

As we emerge from the water, we've got the damp sheen of prehistoric beasts about us. I note her uncompromising integrity as she cuts through a gap in the trees that I'm not sure I would have spotted.

As we walk my body changes. Longer limbs, broad-shouldered with an impressive gait. Six feet or more. Hand spans that would make dresses look like drag but are useful for clearing paths and bearing weight. For the first time in my life, even at this size, it feels okay to follow someone smaller than me. She leads.

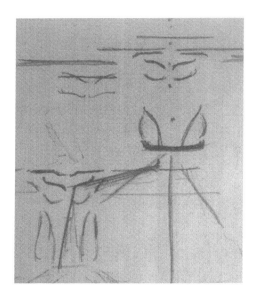

I make her laugh. She laughs. It ripples through me like
permission that I didn't know that I had been seeking. It takes
a minute but I realise this is joy. Proper joy.

As I watch her go it occurs to me that this is no place for tits, or
jugs, or ass. Ass will not help when there are bears.

Having spent a lifetime negotiating with God for body
alterations (an ungrateful waste of prayer) suddenly, my only
want is thicker skin on the soles of my feet so that I can stamp
on snakeheads.

We get to the cabin at night. We sit by candlelight, the lake,
outside, becalmed.

We have to pull wine from the bottle with our hands as Semele
has left us well-stocked but no cocking corkscrew, notoriously
impractical the demigods. We light the fire and listen to the rain.

The faint cracking of twigs underfoot. Others come. From out
the forest. A tribe. Wide-eyed and seeking, we who have felt too
long lost – here, tonight. Once alone, now found. The joy, at
last, in belonging is – [*Smiles, almost tears, the heartbreaking
exhalation of relief of finally finding home.*]

[*A beat starts, the tribe, start to gently stamp – to move – to find a.*
They dance – tribal –
Fire.]

Semele returns and watches, smiling – laughing – ripping the heads off chickens, spitting fig pips, biting into dark tomatoes.

We laugh. And eat. And eat. To answer hunger. For taste, for pleasure. And laugh. And eat. And laugh. And dance. With our bits out and our faces on. And dance.

[*A daft dance. A full-blown funny thing. The idiocy of not needing to look good. When the wine's in you.*]

By the fire we tell our stories; the bonds we broke, the skins we
shed, the fences that we flattened in our panic. Her, pretending
straightness – waking in the night next to men and not being
able to breathe, she'd get in the car and drive a hundred miles to
see her safely over the state line by morning. Me, well-behaved
decades, biting back the tears of not belonging, whilst yet
another family, unspooling dreadfully next door.
But all that is now behind us. The grief is eased.

[*Fire. Fire. Fire. Dance. 'Let the bridges that you burn light
the way.'*
The tribe dissolves. Goes to sleep.]

When our tribe retires. Gloriously exhausted.
She and I – my swimming mate.
Dig our fingers into damp mud.
Birds shriek. Occasional frogs.
Muffled drum of midnight.
With very little ceremony and even less fuss, we fuck.

She knows what she's up to more than I do but whilst new, I'm
not a novice. It turns out, of course, that you do know what
you're doing. You've done it to yourself a thousand times and
how delightful to negotiate your sameness on another and
celebrate it from the outside. That is the only outside there is.
No one is sexy. Everything is sex. There is no looking. There is
only being.

What is nicest, is being allowed to be the right size. With men,
I was always playing small to try and make sense of them
having to mount you. But you're also having to be mother so
you can manage the insecurity of their dick being in open air.
It can be exhausting. Not being allowed to fully fill your own
skin for fear it knocks them, painfully, off their perch. And once
it's done and you try to sleep, I find I never can. Next to men,
I feel like I'm left in the shadow of something. I used to lay
there in the cold for hours.

But when we sleep, she and I, occasionally her head is on my
chest and my arm is slung around her. Later, my bigness, is
curled into the small of her back, the backs of her knees, my

arms seeking harbour in the 'couldn't-give-a-fuck-ness' of her being very much asleep. We are both mothers and both children and somehow it isn't odd, both daughters, both brothers, both friends, both lovers. For the first time in my life I feel like I'm in bed with an ally.

Post-coitally, with her, I feel more whole. Not the semi-devastation that follows sex with men, the land-grab, the Blitzkrieg, the small strange impulse to cry. With her it was an aggregation.

In the morning, we wake, the tribe arrives – we draw a large chalk circle on the forest floor and stand inside it. We feel the possibility of new constructions – systems, schemes and structures – We are making a space conceived entirely by the architecture of our wanting.

[*A chalk circle. A structure. A system. A scheme. For a new world: the whole earth changes its face. Buildings rearrange. Paths are made, miles wide. New arrangements so large you can see them from space.*]

I am happy. For the first time in a long time. I know in my bones that I am happy.

[*During this time: Dolly Parton's 'Light of a Clear Blue Morning' and Todd Baker 'Power of Two'. Dance: Bodylessness /Sameness/Tribe. We all sing. We all dance. It's a celebration. It is joyous; the stars are as big as fists.*]

[*The song ends. The celebration finishes. A new state has been achieved. The new world is built.*]

One night I feel the strange need to go for a walk. She, stranger still, begs me not to. But I get out of bed, a sheet wrapped round my waist, and go all the same.

Little do I know but on a nearby peak, there is a tourist. In clean hiking books and stain-free cargo trousers, with binoculars held to his eyes. He has seen the little plume of smoke rising from our structure.

In a flood of shame, I find myself oddly drawn to this man. Like the colonial dude that took the photograph and stole a soul when he'd been asked, politely not to.

I am being watched but I don't know where from. I can feel it. The experience is acute.
I would slice off great chunks of flesh here and now, if he had handed me a knife.
If she was here, she would say 'give a shit'. She would say, we've got hills to climb and bodies of water to cross.
But I had left her sleeping.

The next thing I remember is the smell of jet fuel; airport runways. Something in the weight of feet on tarmac telling me that I am, once again, resoundingly mortal. Looked at. Patted down. This strange cage so much more visible for having spent some deific time without it.
Enough, perhaps to make you wish, you'd never tasted freedom.

Where is she now? With all her compact pragmatism. I'm not sure I would recognise her if I saw her in the street. How would I know to take her hand and tell her that she's safe? That we were right and it is this that's wrong.

FOUR

DIRECTOR. That's not it.

WRITER. What's not it?

DIRECTOR. It's not – uh… it's not – real. I mean I get what you're trying to do but it's not real.

WRITER. I know it's not real. It's a play.

DIRECTOR. Right. But it needs an ending. We can't leave it there. We're asking people to pay a ticket price, we can't just – all that, isn't –

WRITER. What do you suggest?

–

DIRECTOR. We've invested in the relationship between the writer and the director. That's what you set up at the beginning and it doesn't pay off.

WRITER. The director?

DIRECTOR. It feels – it would be strange if he doesn't return. You expect –

WRITER. You?

DIRECTOR. The audience, dramaturgically – he needs to return. The first scene, has the most energy in it, you know it does. It's the most successful by a long way. It's the best bit of writing.

WRITER. Depending on your definition of 'best'.

DIRECTOR. Dramatic, it's the most dramatic –

WRITER. It's the greatest power struggle, sure. There's the greatest differential in power.

DIRECTOR. Which makes it the most dramatic.

WRITER. Two people, you and me, standing on stage,
   intellectual back-and-forth is dialectic, one oppressing the
   other, it's wordy, it's Stoppard, it's Pinter, it's power
   struggle, it's patriarchy – that's what it is, it's how it's learnt
   and how it's meant to be, it's elitist. It's of an entirely
   different politic to what I'm trying to /

DIRECTOR. / It's good drama. It's what works. It's the
   definition of good drama.

WRITER. Exactly!

DIRECTOR. Stop fucking up the potential of this thing by being
   so bloody petulant all the time. It's a great bit of writing, it's
   got a real shot at the West End – but it can't – it can't go there
   with all this tribal shit in the middle of it. I understand it's an
   experiment, it's – But you're doing yourself a disservice.
   It looks like a lack of confidence in the other stuff. And you
   don't need to lack confidence – You've got to be a bit more of
   a grown-up about it.

WRITER. It's what I wanted to write. The forest, the freedom –
   I – It felt, it was the first time I'd been really happy whilst
   writing something. I felt incredibly sure.

DIRECTOR. That's great.

WRITER. I felt sure!

DIRECTOR. It's not good theatre.

WRITER. You weren't moved?

DIRECTOR. By the running around in the forest?

WRITER. Do you think that's reductive?

DIRECTOR. I wasn't moved.

WRITER. Really?

DIRECTOR. The first scene is better. It's a better bit of work.

WRITER. Do you think that might be about taste. Or
   schooling? Or the fact that your mother didn't like you?

DIRECTOR (*wry smile*). You see, that's what we're after.

WRITER. I'm being serious.

DIRECTOR. That's a shame.

WRITER. Why do you do that smile?

DIRECTOR. What?

WRITER. That wry smile – it – makes it seem like we're on the same team.

DIRECTOR. I guess I'm trying to – woo you.

WRITER. Woo me. How?

DIRECTOR. Make you –

WRITER. What?

DIRECTOR. The best version of yourself.

WRITER. I wouldn't want to be a disappointment.

DIRECTOR. I'm not trying to stop you. I admire the wackiness. I don't dislike the unconventionality. I'm not even, saying cut it out – although if you did it would be –

She turns away.

Anyway – I – I'm just saying it really needs an ending. A revolution isn't worth very much if it has no practical implication. Is it? There's thirty grand of production costs at stake that need to be recouped and currently it feels unfinished.

Beat – she doesn't respond.

Listen, I'm being – I'm not telling you anything you don't already – you know, you know that first scene is the best, it snaps off the page, it's brilliant. No one does that charged – angry – feisty /

WRITER. / Feisty?

DIRECTOR. Thing.

WRITER. I think there's heat in what we just saw.

DIRECTOR. Yeah?

WRITER. The stuff between the writer and director is power play – but there's no – real – heat.

DIRECTOR. I don't agree and I don't think you agree.

They stare.

WRITER. The kind of heat that comes from being very honest.

Pause – we feel the DIRECTOR *should speak but he doesn't.*

DIRECTOR. What's it trying to say? What's it trying to do? In dramatic terms, it's atmospheric but I'm not sure it's *doing* anything.

WRITER. Okay.

DIRECTOR. So?

WRITER. You just let me know what it is you want me to write and I'll write it. You jot it down and I'll type it up. Will that work for you?

DIRECTOR. You know, I get a bit bored of this – I endlessly hand out opportunity and no one is grateful for it, everyone thinks it's their God-given right, it's their *duty*, to be difficult. Do you know how many versions of you I get at my office door every day? I'm offering you a production. That's a lot. That's more than most people get and certainly enough to be grateful for. So just compromise a tiny bit. Or just admit to what you already know is true. Finish the play. Hand it in with a real fucking ending. It has to sell tickets or the whole financial model doesn't work, and if that's too much reality for your delicate artist soul then take a hike. Take it to someone else because I can't listen to this shit any more.

WRITER. I can't end it with a scene between him and her, it would feel like betrayal.

DIRECTOR. Betrayal of what?

WRITER. You really don't see it, do you?

DIRECTOR. I bet you, I bet you the next play will be a male protagonist and good-old fashioned commercial naturalism. I bet you. Because the trend will be over and you don't want to get pigeonholed, it suits you now while the moment is hot because you are well aware of the commercial value of your opposition – but the second it's not cool any more, you'll jump ship quicker than we can blink and you'll be back here with something entertaining like none of this happened at all because more than anything else, just like the rest of us, you fear irrelevance. So – don't pretend this is about anything grander than getting your fucking play on.

WRITER. Takes months, years to get plays on usually. I write about a director and it goes on straight away with the only condition being that we need more director in it.

DIRECTOR. You knew exactly what you were doing. I have to put it on. You know I have to put it on – if I don't, someone else does and it looks even more – you know exactly what the fuck you're doing and it's tantamount to blackmail. All this moralistic, principled, 'it's all about the politics' posturing is bullshit. And it's boring. It's bad theatre. And you fucking know it.

WRITER. Do you know how hard writing a play is?

Beat – she looks for his acknowledgment – he doesn't give it.

Do you know what it is to have to sit down, on your own, to face yourself – every day. Do you know how hard it is? (*Beat.*) So maybe you should stop telling us how it should be done.

DIRECTOR. It's my job. It's what I'm good at. It's what I've spent decades getting really good at.

WRITER. Does it bother you that I slept with a woman?

DIRECTOR. What?

WRITER. When I didn't sleep with you?

DIRECTOR. No.

WRITER. Does it scare you that the future might speak a language that you can't understand?

Small beat.

DIRECTOR. You know what I think? I think all this breaking-form shit is an intellectual exercise that lets you jump out of whatever difficult and uncomfortable thing just getting on and writing the scene would lead you in to. You know the first scene is the best. You know there's something between that writer and director that people want to watch, that people want to bite down on, and you're a coward, you fly off to feminist manifestos and dancing in the fucking woods because you're scared of what you might actually want to say if you followed it through.

Stand-off – breath.

WRITER. Which is?

DIRECTOR. Sleeping with girls is the same thing. It's a holiday, it's a hobby.

WRITER. It was a peace and contentment that I've never – that – since I lost… it has crucified me.

DIRECTOR. It's a holiday from what scares you and you've fashioned a fucking revolution out of it. It's fraudulent.

WRITER. And this is – ? (*Indicates something between the two of them.*) This is what? Real life?

DIRECTOR. In my experience, outrage is only ever a cover for something deeper. Only time I've ever been outraged – I was really just asking someone to love me more.

WRITER. You think this whole moment is about women seeking your approval?

Pause – DIRECTOR doesn't respond.

When I came up to your office and you went to get the contract. I saw – on your desk – that photograph. She's laughing – holding a ball, this little blonde bob. (*Beat.*) You never talk about her.

DIRECTOR. Don't I?

WRITER. Why don't you ever talk about your daughter?

DIRECTOR. I do. All the time. (*Beat.*) Just not to you.

WRITER. Why not to me?

Pause. Breath from both. Something fragile hangs about.

DIRECTOR. I've got a meeting I need to get to. You need to finish it. I can't sell tickets to Maria von Trapp trumped up in wode, it just won't sell.

WRITER. When I got back. I had felt so happy there. Such an amazing sense of belonging. When I got back. The – loneliness, there was something so bleak about. I feel like I have no tribe. There's nothing mythic in this city and it breaks me. I – I feel so un-found and there I was so – I was so… and you – for all the fighting and the – you are the only thing that makes sense. That makes me feel like I have a home – you are my size, you have to –

DIRECTOR. What?

WRITER. Artists have to feel safe. If you want them to make art. We have to feel – emotionally – safe. We – I, need to belong to something. The places you have to go – the things you have to feel and think are… going there – can get… dangerous. And you're so often alone and I've got no one and you do and… /

DIRECTOR. / It's just a play.

WRITER. Not the good ones. They're not just /

DIRECTOR. / It's not my job to look after you.

WRITER. I know that. I just. It costs so much. And there's nothing – to.

Beat.

DIRECTOR. You write the ending – a good ending, a proper ending, we can make you some real money. Money fosters confidence and what's art if not an act of confidence?

WRITER. When I was there. I felt so sure. I felt /

DIRECTOR. / You wouldn't survive in poverty for a second.
Come on – this is the world, this is the real world. It's an
industry, it's a business – it's a /

WRITER. / It might suit you to call it a profession but it was
never meant to be – it was meant to be a dedication, a
calling. Not for mortgages and pay cheques and career
progression, it was for God, it was an offering. It was
Dionysus, it was giving thanks, it was catharsis, it was Holy
Fire. But now it belongs to you because you've paid for it
and it's judged on whether it will shift tickets.

DIRECTOR. I'm trying to make you great.

WRITER. So, I have you to thank? For expecting so much of me?

DIRECTOR. In part, yes.

WRITER. I didn't earn it on my own?

DIRECTOR. I have helped you more than anyone else has.
Haven't I?

Pause – she doesn't respond.

Haven't I? Right. So maybe a little gratitude and humility
would –

WRITER. Thank you. Thank you for all of the opportunity
you've given me.

Weirdly long silence.

DIRECTOR. I do it because I think you're good. I do it because
I think you are exceptional. It scares me how good you are.
(*Pause.*) I have a meeting I need to be at, I – (*Gets halfway
to the door, stops.*) I know you suffer. The idea of anything
happening to – If you stopped, I – Let me do what I can do,
the only thing I can do – to make you safe.

WRITER. Money?

DIRECTOR. It matters.

WRITER. But that's not safe at all.

DIRECTOR. Of course, it is. Of course – it is.

WRITER. Courage. Courage is what makes you safe.

He turns – they look at one another.

DIRECTOR. Get it finished. Get it finished or it doesn't go on.

FIVE

WRITER *and* FEMALE ACTOR *stand whilst a set gets moved on around them.*

It's the West End version of the apartment from Part Two. It's high-end, smart, glitzy – the commercialism sings out through the reserved luxury of it, the seamlessness. WRITER *and* GIRLFRIEND *look ill at ease, standing static, as it's arranged around them. We should recognise* GIRLFRIEND *as a version of the partner* WRITER *speaks about in Part Four. Make-up and costume do a real number on the* WRITER *and the* GIRLFRIEND. *They look like hot, hipster, versions of their previous selves, as does the flat. We should, if possible, get the sense the* DIRECTOR *has directed the scene.*

Curtain up.

WRITER *enters the flat.*

GIRLFRIEND. You have a good day?

WRITER (*optimism*). Yeah, it was okay.

GIRLFRIEND. Didn't get bored?

WRITER. No. It's nice. How was yours?

GIRLFRIEND *kisses* WRITER. WRITER *takes her face and kisses her back.*

GIRLFRIEND. Can't complain.

They smile.

Sit – we're eating.

GIRLFRIEND *goes into the kitchen.* WRITER *lays the table.* GIRLFRIEND *re-enters with take-out boxes on a tray.*

WRITER. You. [*You spoil me.*]

GIRLFRIEND. I know.

WRITER. I got bread.

> WRITER *hands her a plate*, GIRLFRIEND *puts curry on it.*
> GIRLFRIEND *hands* WRITER *the plate.* GIRLFRIEND
> *gives herself some – they sit and eat – there's little ceremony
> but a lot of contentment.* GIRLFRIEND *takes one mouthful,
> notices that the candle isn't lit and gets up to do it.*

Did they sort out the boiler in the bar?

GIRLFRIEND. The guy came but said he needed a part he
didn't have so he's got to come back tomorrow. You want
a bhaji?

WRITER. Nuh-uh.

GIRLFRIEND. You love a bhaji.

WRITER. I'm fine.

GIRLFRIEND. You dunk it in the mango chutney.

WRITER. Don't want it. So is he coming back tomorrow?

GIRLFRIEND. Yeah. We're having to wash all the glasses by
boiling kettles, it's a fucking ball-ache.

WRITER. I'll come and help you tomorrow if you want.

GIRLFRIEND. Yeah?

WRITER. I fancy doing something – manual. For a bit. Sort my
head out.

GIRLFRIEND. Glad we can help.

WRITER. What?

GIRLFRIEND. Nothing.

WRITER. What do you mean by that?

GIRLFRIEND. Just funny when you use my job as a holiday
for your tired brain.

WRITER. No, it's just weird, it's just all me, two years of
writing and then I just hand it in, there's no – there's no
anyone else. It's –

GIRLFRIEND. It's what you wanted.

WRITER. I'm not saying I don't like it. Just be nice to work in a team.

GIRLFRIEND *gets up and goes through to the kitchen.*

What are you doing?

GIRLFRIEND. Getting the mango, so you can dunk your bhaji.

WRITER (*shouting after her*). I said I didn't want one.

GIRLFRIEND. You have a meeting with anyone today?

WRITER. Because I don't want a bhaji?

GIRLFRIEND (*shouting through*). Last time he tried to convince you to write something for him you bought a new pair of shoes.

WRITER. I needed new shoes.

GIRLFRIEND (*re-entering, sitting down, opening the mango chutney*). Which you've never worn, thank God, because I swore to myself very early on in life that I would never go out with someone in loafers.

WRITER. They're not loafers.

GIRLFRIEND (*dunking and eating a bhaji*). They are loafers. They are tan loafers and they are unacceptable.

GIRLFRIEND *takes the other half of her bhaji – leans across, with it dunked in mango and gives it (in a non-sexualised but enjoyable way) to the* WRITER.

You've worked so hard to leave your loafer life behind, it would be so sad if you turned back now.

GIRLFRIEND *is checking her phone, engrossed.* WRITER *watches.*

WRITER. What is it?

GIRLFRIEND. The boiler guy has showed up. That's nice of him.

WRITER. It's late.

GIRLFRIEND. I know. What a nice guy. Stuff like that, man. You want beer?

WRITER. Yes.

WRITER *watches her partner head into the kitchen for beer.*

(*Not loud enough for her to hear.*) I love you.

GIRLFRIEND *comes back out with two beers.*

GIRLFRIEND. What?

WRITER. Pass it here?

WRITER *puts her hand out for the beer and opens it.*

GIRLFRIEND. What did you say?

WRITER (*having to drink the beer quickly to stop it frothing over*). Mmhm – hm – hm mm, that's nice, what is that?

GIRLFRIEND. Smuttynose.

WRITER (*still dealing with the froth*). Hm?

GIRLFRIEND. It's called Smuttynose.

WRITER *goes over and kisses the* GIRLFRIEND. *Picks her up – she's small – she wraps her legs around.*

Hey, hey – wait, no – my Smuttynose!

The WRITER *ignores the fact that it's spilling, laughs –* GIRLFRIEND *manages, just about, to get the can of beer down before the* WRITER *lies her back on the couch. The sex is obscured from the audience – behind the sofa – we can hear it, but barely – but we can't see anything. It's good sex, the best we've seen. They know what is good and they get it done.*

GIRLFRIEND *gets up – pulls her trousers back on – kisses* WRITER, *picks up her beer – takes a slurp – looks down at the sofa, at the* WRITER *who is laying with her hands behind her head.*

You're such a John.

WRITER. What's a John?

GIRLFRIEND. The kind of guy that puts his hands behind his head like that after he makes someone come. You want a high-five?

WRITER (*laughing*). Sure.

GIRLFRIEND *offers her hand – high in the air –* WRITER *has to lean up.*

Awh – stomach muscles –

WRITER *reaches for the hand – gets it – they high-five, she collapses back.* GIRLFRIEND *laughs, drinks more beer.* GIRLFRIEND *goes to sit in one chair, her feet up on another chair – drinks her beer, checks her phone.* WRITER *watches her.*

Will you marry me?

GIRLFRIEND. What? What did you just say?

WRITER. I said, will you marry me?

GIRLFRIEND. Don't do that.

WRITER. What?

GIRLFRIEND. Just because you're in some fucking post-coital glow. That's not cool. Don't do that.

GIRLFRIEND *goes back to her phone.* WRITER, *slightly burnt, gets up and clears the plates away, into the kitchen. She comes back out.* GIRLFRIEND *is still nonchalantly on her phone. She watches.*

WRITER. I feel like I'm your dad sometimes.

GIRLFRIEND. What? Why?

WRITER. I don't know. Like I'm in slacks and a cardigan and I'm watching you have fun before I retire to my office and get some work done.

WRITER *is standing,* GIRLFRIEND *looks up at her, from her seat.*

GIRLFRIEND. That's messed up.

WRITER. Is it?

GIRLFRIEND. Do you want children?

WRITER. Right now?

GIRLFRIEND. Do you?

WRITER. Why are we talking about children?

GIRLFRIEND. You just started chatting about it. Do you want children?

WRITER. Not from my own body, no.

Beat.

GIRLFRIEND. You wouldn't mind if I had some from mine?

WRITER. How would you get them in there?

GIRLFRIEND. We'd get one in there.

WRITER. How?

GIRLFRIEND. You mean, practically how do we /

WRITER. / Who?

GIRLFRIEND. So that there's genetic code from both of us, so it's shared, we could ask your brother.

Very small beat.

WRITER. My brother is very unlikely to put a child into a lesbian.

GIRLFRIEND. It wouldn't be his child, it would be ours.

WRITER. It would look like him.

GIRLFRIEND. It would look like you.

WRITER. It would be his child, in you. That would be the state of things.

GIRLFRIEND. So that's a no?

WRITER. I. I'm not averse to having them – around. I can see them being – around. In here. About the place.

GIRLFRIEND. Like – animals?

WRITER. Sure, not unlike – although I don't really like dogs.

GIRLFRIEND. We could get a dog?

WRITER. I don't want a dog. They're unpredictable – I don't like the way when you're reading they're about all the time, it makes me really tense. They could do anything at any time. They don't just sit and read.

GIRLFRIEND. Dogs?

WRITER. I just – It's nice to be able to have quiet when you want it. I sort of need to have quiet when I need it.

GIRLFRIEND. Right.

WRITER. Okay.

GIRLFRIEND. That's fine.

> GIRLFRIEND *goes back to playing on her phone.* WRITER *is slightly confused, she's not entirely sure what just happened there.*

WRITER. Can I go down on you?

GIRLFRIEND. I'm doing emails.

WRITER. That's fine.

> GIRLFRIEND *continues with her emails.* WRITER *with her back to us goes to put her head between the* GIRLFRIEND*'s legs.*

> I need to take your jeans off.

GIRLFRIEND. It's cold. I – Can't you – You can totally make me come without me having to take my jeans off. You totally can. I believe in you.

> WRITER *gets down on her knees.*

> GIRLFRIEND *pats* WRITER's *head.*

> WRITER *noses and pushes, with hands and face – into the* GIRLFRIEND*'s crotch. The* GIRLFRIEND, *relatively*

quickly – puts the phone down – puts her hand on the
WRITER*'s head. Pulls the* WRITER *up to face height and*
kisses her. The WRITER *is still kneeling between the*
GIRLFRIEND*'s legs but now sitting up, the* GIRLFRIEND
is on the chair so they are face height. They stop kissing and
GIRLFRIEND *takes* WRITER*'s face in her hands.*
GIRLFRIEND *seems taller, bigger, overseeing for a second.*

GIRLFRIEND *kisses* WRITER *on the forehead, smooths*
down the hair on the top of her head.

WRITER *bows her head slightly – lets her hair be played*
with.

WRITER. I want to.

GIRLFRIEND. Really?

WRITER. Yes I think so.

GIRLFRIEND. With the /

WRITER. / Yes. I think so. I – Yes, let's, okay. I still feel
fundamentally opposed to prosthetics, I just don't think we
can make anything better than what we were born with but
seeing as you're an advocate – I don't see why *not*.

During this speech, GIRLFRIEND*, has gone to get her*
backpack – she's rooting around inside it.

– it's in your bag?

GIRLFRIEND. Yeah.

WRITER. You keep it with you?

GIRLFRIEND. At all times.

WRITER. ? What.

GIRLFRIEND. I knew you'd say yes eventually.

WRITER. And so you keep it in your bag?

GIRLFRIEND. Take your trousers off.

WRITER. I. Jesus. There's curry on the table.

GIRLFRIEND. Take them off. I need to wash it.

GIRLFRIEND *goes into the kitchen.*

WRITER. Oh God, why? This is – You know what, actually no – This whole thing is – Why do you need to wash it? What have you been using it for that you need to wash it?

GIRLFRIEND (*shouting through*). Nothing, it's just been in my bag with those chick-pea crisps you left in there.

GIRLFRIEND *comes back out of the kitchen holding a pegging penis – it's not a strap on – it's pretty sculptural – it's held inside one person and offers a dick to be used on the other person. It has real presence though. The object of it very much sucks all the air out of the room. It should be a dark colour – dark blue or black – not pink or purple or red.*

Pause.

WRITER. It's spotless.

GIRLFRIEND. You don't want it with crumbs on. One doesn't want it with crumbs on.

WRITER. I'm not sure one wants it at all.

GIRLFRIEND. It's going to be fine.

WRITER. Hm.

GIRLFRIEND. You'll *be* fine.

WRITER *goes over to the sofa, takes her trousers off and lies back. It's all very slow and slightly suspect.*

You might have to put your beer down.

GIRLFRIEND *takes the beer from* WRITER.

WRITER *lies back on the sofa.*

GIRLFRIEND *takes her own trousers off – arranges herself over the* WRITER, *inserts the object and is about to begin. Beat.* WRITER *looks up at the* GIRLFRIEND. *Suddenly the* WRITER *gets out of there as fast as she can. She's up, trousers on, over to the table, rests both hands on it, braces herself against it, bites back tears of not belonging. Tries to breathe.*

GIRLFRIEND *just sits, quietly, looking in the* WRITER*'s direction, gently, kindly – and lets whatever the tension is, whatever the ball of pain is, unfurl a bit.*

She rests both hands on the table. Looks down at the plates. Tries to breathe.

What's wrong?

–

We don't have to use it.

WRITER. Okay.

–

–

–

GIRLFRIEND. Is that it?

WRITER. What?

GIRLFRIEND. That you don't want to use it?

WRITER. Sure. I. Uh.

–

–

–

I could use it.

GIRLFRIEND. You could use it. You've never used it before. It takes a bit of –

WRITER. I can use it. I'm sure I can use it.

GIRLFRIEND. Okay.

WRITER. Yeah?

GIRLFRIEND. That's fine.

GIRLFRIEND *holds the object out to* WRITER. WRITER *comes over and takes it.*

WRITER. It's heavier than you'd think.

GIRLFRIEND. A substantial mass.

It's handed over.

GIRLFRIEND *lies back – she disappears to us.* WRITER *arranges herself – puts it in, braces herself against the sofa – there's no connection, the concentration is all logistical – and focused on the groin area.*

You can still look at me.

WRITER. Sorry.

GIRLFRIEND. Are you okay?

WRITER. Yeah, yeah – I'm fine. Yep, I'm fine. Thanks.

GIRLFRIEND. Are you /

WRITER. / Can you stop talking?

WRITER *gets going. We don't hear anything from the* GIRLFRIEND.

Silence from the GIRLFRIEND. *The* WRITER *starts enjoying it. She's really going for it – there's something strangely aggressive about it – she's in the zone, it's all her, the* GIRLFRIEND *has all but evaporated. The* WRITER *comes. The* GIRLFRIEND *does not.*

The GIRLFRIEND *gets up, does her trousers up, picks up the remaining curry and clears it away into the kitchen and all without saying anything. The* WRITER *sits in a sort of guilty-feeling half-daze, looking for reassurance from the* GIRLFRIEND, *maybe from the room – but doesn't get it.*

(*Shouting through to* GIRLFRIEND *in the kitchen.*) Are you okay?

No response.

WRITER *stands, does up her jeans.*

Are you okay in there?

Pause.

GIRLFRIEND *comes out of the kitchen – holding a tray with a pot of tea and two cups on it – it's unexpected and strangely wife-like.*

GIRLFRIEND. Sure.

GIRLFRIEND *puts the tea down on the table,* WRITER *watches, finding it odd.*

WRITER. What are you doing?

GIRLFRIEND. I thought we could have some tea. It's warm. My mum gave me some posh orange-blossom-tea-leaf stuff when I went to see her. You put it in this little ball with holes in it but it means you've got to use a pot. You want some tea?

WRITER. Um.

GIRLFRIEND. It smells amazing, smell that –

GIRLFRIEND *offers the tea pot to be sniffed.* WRITER *doesn't want to sniff it.*

WRITER. I might get a beer.

GIRLFRIEND. They were the only two I had. Want a biscuit?

WRITER. I don't want sweet.

GIRLFRIEND. God, I do.

GIRLFRIEND *sits at the table, pours herself a tea, adds lots of milk, sort of sucks on a sugary biscuit, she really pays attention to it – licks all the sugar off, eats round the sides, it's ravenous but also, oddly – kid-like.*

WRITER *watches her.*

Really yummy. Yum scrum in my tum.

Something breaks in the WRITER *– something awful.*

WRITER. Have I done something?

Looking up at her with big kid eyes.

GIRLFRIEND. Hm?

WRITER. To you?

GIRLFRIEND. To me? No? Why?

WRITER. I feel like I've done something terrible.

–

–

–

GIRLFRIEND (*still weirdly involved in her cookie*). Have you ever fucked someone taller than you?

WRITER. No.

GIRLFRIEND. A girl?

WRITER. You're the only girl, I've ever /

GIRLFRIEND. / And you don't think you'd fuck a tall girl or a white girl? Or just the small ones?

WRITER. I. I don't know why but, um.

GIRLFRIEND. Can you imagine fucking a girl bigger than you?

Pause.

WRITER. No.

GIRLFRIEND. No?

WRITER (*revulsion*). It's horrible. The idea of that. It's. Sorry. I don't like it.

GIRLFRIEND. But you're tall.

–

–

–

–

The WRITER *watches the* GIRLFRIEND *nibble on the cookie with childish delight.*

Someone at the pub this evening told this fucking insane story about Picasso, when he was painting *Guernica*, he was up this ladder and he was in the middle of painting and these two women that he was fucking at the same time were having a fight at the bottom of the ladder, they were wrestling, they drew blood. And he just keeps painting, the whole time – he's painting – the screaming mother, the dead – (*Takes a bite of biscuit.*) and the horror and the – and he's just – (*Imitates. It's kid-like – it's cute.*) Dum di dum – (*Takes a drag of an imaginary fag.*) dum di dum dum – (*Does a few strokes of painting.*) dum di dum dum – (*Takes a sip of imaginary wine.*) dum di dum dum whilst these two women are ripping flesh off each other beneath him. Mental. Do you want a biscuit?

A flash of the image of Picasso's Guernica *covers the stage.*

WRITER *stares – horrified, haunted.*

Curtain down.

End.